IT'S TIME TO EAT BUTTON MUSHROOMS

It's Time to Eat BUTTON MUSHROOMS

Walter the Educator

Silent King Books
A WhichHead Entertainment Imprint

Copyright © 2024 by Walter the Educator

All rights reserved. No part of this book may be reproduced in any manner whatsoever without written per- mission except in the case of brief quotations embodied in critical articles and reviews.

First Printing, 2024

Disclaimer

This book is a literary work; the story is not about specific persons, locations, situations, and/or circumstances unless mentioned in a historical context. Any resemblance to real persons, locations, situations, and/or circumstances is coincidental. This book is for entertainment and informational purposes only. The author and publisher offer this information without warranties expressed or implied. No matter the grounds, neither the author nor the publisher will be accountable for any losses, injuries, or other damages caused by the reader's use of this book. The use of this book acknowledges an understanding and acceptance of this disclaimer.

It's Time to Eat BUTTON MUSHROOMS is a collectible early learning book by Walter the Educator suitable for all ages belonging to Walter the Educator's Time to Eat Book Series. Collect more books at WaltertheEducator.com

USE THE EXTRA SPACE TO TAKE NOTES AND DOCUMENT YOUR MEMORIES

BUTTON MUSHROOMS

It's time to eat, so come on in,

It's Time to Eat Button Mushrooms

Button mushrooms, round and thin.

Soft and smooth, so small and white,

They're ready to give your taste buds delight.

Found in forests or fields so green,

Mushrooms grow where they can't be seen.

Farmers pick them, fresh and neat,

Now they're here, so let's eat!

Chop them up or leave them whole,

Mushrooms make a tasty bowl.

In a salad or on some bread,

Mushrooms fill your tummy instead.

Sauté them gently, watch them sizzle,

Or add them to a soup that'll make you giggle.

Mix them in pasta, or bake them with cheese,

Button mushrooms are sure to please.

It's Time to Eat
Button Mushrooms

They're full of flavor, mild and sweet,

A little veggie that's fun to eat.

On a pizza or in a stew,

Mushrooms have so much to do!

A sprinkle of salt, a dash of spice,

Mushrooms always taste so nice.

With their little caps, they stand so proud,

In every dish, they're cheered by the crowd.

Button mushrooms are good for you,

Full of nutrients through and through.

For energy and a healthy way,

They help you smile all through the day.

Take a bite and feel the fun,

Mushrooms are loved by everyone.

They're soft and chewy, light and mild,

It's Time to Eat
Button Mushrooms

Perfect for any hungry child.

So let's say thank you, mushrooms dear,

For bringing us joy and lots of cheer.

It's time to eat, let's dig right in,

Button mushrooms are a win-win-win!

Now clap your hands, give a big hooray,

Button mushrooms save the day.

Tiny and tasty, full of surprise,

It's Time to Eat
Button Mushrooms

Mushrooms are magic in every bite, no lies!

ABOUT THE CREATOR

Walter the Educator is one of the pseudonyms for Walter Anderson. Formally educated in Chemistry, Business, and Education, he is an educator, an author, a diverse entrepreneur, and he is the son of a disabled war veteran. "Walter the Educator" shares his time between educating and creating. He holds interests and owns several creative projects that entertain, enlighten, enhance, and educate, hoping to inspire and motivate you. Follow, find new works, and stay up to date with Walter the Educator™

at WaltertheEducator.com

Milton Keynes UK
Ingram Content Group UK Ltd.
UKHW010227111224
452348UK00011B/547